THE WHITE STONES

You are on a ferry going to the island of Skaran in Ireland. You are an archaeologist and you want to study the very old white stones on the island – they are 4, 500 years old. But on the ferry, you meet a woman. 'The people on the island don't like archaeologists,' she says.

After you arrive on the island, you drive your car down a small road. There are some trees next to the road, and suddenly one tree begins to move. It falls down in front of your car and you stop quickly. 'Is there somebody behind the trees?' you think. What do you do next? Do you go to the trees and look for somebody, or do you move the tree? Be careful – there is only one way to find the answer to the mystery of the white stones.

This is an interactive story. You can choose what part of the story to read next. Follow the numbers at the end of each section.

OXFORD BOOKWORMS LIBRARY

Thriller & Adventure

The White Stones

Starter (250 headwords)

LESTER VAUGHAN

The White Stones

Illustrated by
David Cuzik

OXFORD UNIVERSITY PRESS

OXFORD
UNIVERSITY PRESS

Great Clarendon Street, Oxford OX2 6DP

Oxford University Press is a department of the University of Oxford.
It furthers the University's objective of excellence in research, scholarship,
and education by publishing worldwide in

Oxford New York

Auckland Cape Town Dar es Salaam Hong Kong Karachi
Kuala Lumpur Madrid Melbourne Mexico City Nairobi
New Delhi Shanghai Taipei Toronto

With offices in

Argentina Austria Brazil Chile Czech Republic France Greece
Guatemala Hungary Italy Japan Poland Portugal Singapore
South Korea Switzerland Thailand Turkey Ukraine Vietnam

OXFORD and OXFORD ENGLISH are registered trade marks of
Oxford University Press in the UK and in certain other countries

This edition © Oxford University Press 2008

The moral rights of the author have been asserted

Database right Oxford University Press (maker)

First published in Oxford Bookworms 2000

4 6 8 10 9 7 5 3

ISBN: 978 0 19 423431 3

Printed in Hong Kong

Word count (main text): 1850

For more information on the Oxford Bookworms Library, visit
www.oup.com/bookworms

CONTENTS

The White Stones

1 Your name is Chris Ellison and you are from London in England. You are on a ferry. The ferry is going to the island of Skaran in Ireland. You are sitting next to a woman. She smiles.

'Are you on holiday?' she asks.

'No,' you say. 'I'm an archaeologist. I want to study the megalithic stones on Skaran. The stones are very interesting. They're very old. But we don't know much about them.'

The woman stops smiling. 'The people on the island don't like archaeologists,' she says.

■ *Go to* **11**.

You walk to the stones. There are nine big stones and one small stone. Two of the stones are very big and have another stone on top.

You look at the small stone. It is red on top.

■ *Go to 34.*

 You try to hit the man but the man hits you first.
■ *Go to 24.*

You walk around the hill. You see a red car behind the hill. There are some boxes in the car.

■ *You go to the old house. Go to* **18**.

 You see that the liquid is coming out of a hole under the car.

■ *You phone a garage. Go to* **32**.

■ *You drive the car to your home. Go to* **19**.

6 You get in your car. You look at more megalithic stones and tombs in the north of the island. They are beautiful in the evening. There are always tombs near the megalithic stones. It is late when you arrive home.

The next day you go to the town of Langrun. You go to some shops and buy some things. What do you do next?

■ *You go home. Go to* **16.**
■ *You go to the Stones of Clayonag. Go to* **20.**

7 You drive slowly down the hill. Ten minutes later you look behind you. You cannot see the red car.

You go past a village. Then you go down a hill to Clayonag. You see a lot of megalithic stones near the sea. It is very beautiful. You stop your car and get out.

■ *Go to 34.*

8 You go the village and you ask some people about the megalithic stones. Nobody wants to talk about them.

■ *You go home. Go to 28.*

■ *You go back to Clayonag. Go to 34.*

9 You look through the door of the tomb. At the back of the tomb there is a stone table. The sun is shining on the table.

■ *Go to 27.*

10 You go to the village and find a policeman. You tell him about the things that are happening to you.

He says, 'People in the village don't like archaeologists because they take our treasures. Perhaps you need to go home to London.'

■ *You go to the old house. Go to 16.*

■ *You look at more stones on the island. Go to 6.*

11 Half an hour later, the ferry stops at the island. You get in your car and drive off the ferry. You drive the car down a small road. In front of you, there are some trees next to the road. One of the trees begins to move. You stop your car quickly. The tree falls in front of your car.

You get out of your car.

'Is there somebody behind the trees?' you ask. What do you do?

■ *You go to the trees and look for somebody. Go to **23**.*
■ *You move the tree from the road. Go to **33**.*

12 You drive very fast but the road is not very good. Your car leaves the road. Then everything goes black.

■ *Go to 24.*

13 You go into the tomb. You see some pictures of knives on the wall. You hear a noise. Everything goes dark. You go to the door. You cannot open it.

'Open the door!' you shout, but nobody comes.

You are afraid. You wait for a very long time but nobody comes.

■ *You go to the back of the tomb. Go to 17.*

■ *You stay near the door. Go to 26.*

14 The American woman walks nearer to you. Suddenly a megalithic stone begins to move. The stone is behind the woman. She does not see that the stone is moving.

'Look!' you say. 'The stone is falling!'

She smiles. 'I'm not stupid, you know,' she says.

She does not look behind her. The megalithic stone makes a lot of noise. It falls on the woman.

You see the man with the long black hair. He is coming down the road. When he sees the woman under the stone, he runs away.

■ *Go to* **29.**

15 You drive to your house and get out of your car. The American woman is standing near your house. She is smiling.

'Would you like to go the Stones of Clayonag tomorrow?' she asks. 'I can't go with you but it's an interesting and important day. It's June 21. It's the longest day of the year. A lot of people go to Clayonag every year. You must go there early in the morning.'

'Thank you,' you say. You go into your house.

■ *Go to 21.*

16 You drive home. When you are near your house, a big stone hits the windscreen of your car. You stop quickly. You get out. Behind you there is a tall man with long black hair. He is running towards you.

■ *You run away. Go to **31**.*
■ *You hit the man. Go to **3**.*

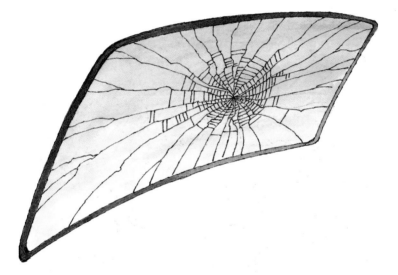

17 You go to the back of the tomb. There is a stone table there. Near the table is a big stone. You take the stone and you go back to the door. You hit the door with the stone. You break the door and you get out of the tomb.

■ *Go to **28**.*

18 When you are near the old house, you meet a woman with blond hair. 'Hello,' she says. 'Are you staying at the old house?'

'Yes,' you say. 'I'm renting it for six weeks.'

'My name's Sarah. I'm staying at the new house,' she says. 'I'm on holiday here. I'm from Los Angeles in America. Are you on holiday?'

'No,' you say, 'I'm an archaeologist. I want to study the megalithic stones on the island.'

'How interesting! I don't know anything about those things,' she says.

■ *You go to the old house. Go to 30.*

19 You drive the car. When you are going down a hill, you cannot stop the car. Your car hits a tree.

■ *Go to 24.*

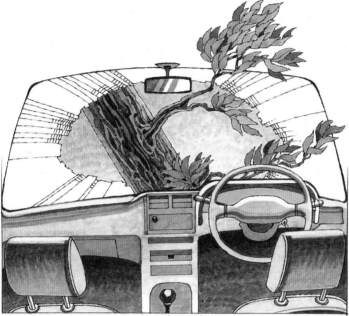

20 You go to the Stones of Clayonag. You look at the stones and wait but nothing happens. You go home late.

For the next two weeks you go around the island and look at the megalithic stones. Nothing more happens to you. You do not find the answer to the mystery.

■ *Go to 1 and try again.*

21 The next day you get up very early. You drive to the Stones of Clayonag. When you arrive, you see a lot of cars. You get out of your car and walk to the tomb. There are a lot of people near the tomb. They are looking at the sun, and waiting.

Slowly the sun comes up. The sun shines between the two big stones. It shines into the door of the tomb. When this happens, the people begin to sing.

■ *You look through the door of the tomb. Go to* **9**.
■ *You do not look through the door. Go to* **27**.

You go to the sea. It is beautiful but you do not see any people or megalithic stones.

You go back to the tomb. You think you see a man. He is behind one of the megalithic stones.

■ *Go to 34.*

 You run into the trees. You see a tall man with long black hair. He runs away. You go back to your car.

■ *Go to 33.*

24 When you open your eyes, you are in a bed in a white room. A woman is looking at you. 'Hello,' she says. 'I'm Doctor O'Connor. Everything is all right. You're in hospital.'

A week later you leave the hospital. You do not know the answer to the mystery.

■ *Go back to* **1** *and start again!*

25 You stop your car. You look behind you. The red car stops too.

■ *Go to* **7**.

26 You stay next to the door. Four hours later the door opens. You go out of the tomb. It is dark. There is nobody near the tomb. You think you see a man. He is running towards the road.

■ *You get in your car and drive home. Go to 15.*

27 An hour later everybody gets in their cars and leaves Clayonag. You go to your car. There is some liquid on the road under the car.

■ *You look under the car. Go to 5.*

■ *You drive the car to your home. Go to 19.*

■ *You phone a garage. Go to 32.*

28 You go home. When you are near the old house, you see a red car. There is a man near the car. He is tall with long black hair. He is with the old American woman. When he sees you, he gets into his car. He drives away.
■ *Go to* **15**.

29 You phone the police. They arrive ten minutes later. The police look at the stone. 'After all these years, why does the stone fall now?' says a policeman.

'It's a mystery,' you say.

The police move the stone and take the woman to hospital. The police arrest the man with the long hair and the woman from the ferry.

Thanks to you the treasures of the island are now safe and the archaeologists can study the old tombs.

30 You go to the old house. There is some writing on the door of the house. It says, 'Go back to London, Ellison! We don't want you on our island.'

The next day you drive to Clayonag in the north of the island. There are a lot of megalithic stones in Clayonag. You drive up a small road. The road is bad. You look behind you and you see a red car. You drive fast. The red car goes fast. You go down a hill.

■ *You drive slower. Go to* **7**.

■ *You drive very fast. Go to* **12**.

■ *You stop your car. Go to* **25**.

31 You run through some trees. You come to a small road. You run down the road and you see your house and the megalithic stone. There are some boxes in a car near the stone. You go to a box and look into it. There are cups and knives in the box. They are very old. You think they are about 4,000 years old. Now you see a hole in the hill. The hill is a megalithic tomb. Somebody is taking things from the tomb.

You hear a noise and you see Sarah, the American woman. She is coming out of the tomb with a knife in her hand.

■ *You do not move. Go to* **14.**

■ *You run away. Go to* **35.**

32 You walk to a village and phone a garage. Three hours later a man comes. He works on the car for a long time. At four o'clock the car is ready.

- ■ *You find a policeman. Go to **10**.*
- ■ *You drive home. Go to **16**.*
- ■ *You look at more megalithic stones and tombs. Go to **6**.*

33 You move the tree from the road. You get in your car and continue down the road. Five minutes later, you see two houses. There is an old house and a new house. You are renting the old house.

There is a small hill near the houses. There are megalithic stones around the hill.

'This is a nice place to live,' you think.

You get out of your car. You look at the stone. You think it is about 4,000 years old.

■ *You walk around the hill. Go to* **4.**

■ *You go to the old house. Go to* **18.**

34 Near the megalithic stones is a hill. You walk to the hill. There is a door in the hill. On the door there is some writing. It says, 'Megalithic Tomb. 4,500 Years Old.' The door is open. You look in the tomb. It is very dark.

- ■ *You walk to the stones. Go to* **2**.
- ■ *You go to the village and ask about the stones. Go to* **8**.
- ■ *You go into the tomb. Go to* **13**.
- ■ *You go to the sea. Go to* **22**.

35 You run away but you fall on the boxes.
- ■ *Go to* **14**.

GLOSSARY

archaeologist a person who studies old things

arrest *(vb)* when the police take somebody to the police station

continue *(vb)* when you do not stop doing something, or you start again

garage a place where people work on cars

hole an opening in something; when you take a stone out of the ground you leave a hole

holiday a day or days when you do not go to work or school

megalith a big stone about 3,000–5,000 years old

mystery something you do not understand, you do not know the answer to

rent *(vb)* give somebody money so that you can stay in a house

safe not in danger – nothing bad can happen

shout *(vb)* speak loudly; when someone cannot hear you very well you need to shout

stone a hard thing you normally find in the ground

study *(vb)* learn about things; students study at school

treasure a very important thing; you can get a lot of money for it

The White Stones

ACTIVITIES

ACTIVITIES

Before Reading

1 Look at the front and back cover of the book. Choose the correct answers to these questions.

1 Where can you find these megalithic stones?
   a ☐ Mexico.
   b ☐ Ireland.
   c ☐ Japan.

2 How old are the stones?
   a ☐ 1,500 years old.
   b ☐ 2,500 years old.
   c ☐ 4,500 years old.

3 What are the stones for, do you think?
   a ☐ Nobody knows.
   b ☐ They are the walls of an old building.
   c ☐ A place for dead people.

2 Guess what happens in the story.

	YES	NO
a Somebody doesn't want Chris to study the stones.	☐	☐
b Somebody wants to take the stones to America.	☐	☐
c Somebody on the island is killing people.	☐	☐
d The stones can kill people.	☐	☐

While Reading

1 Read the first parts of the story (1, 11 and 33).
Are these sentences true (T) or false (F)?

	T	F
1 Chris Ellison is from America.	☐	☐
2 The megalithic stones are in England.	☐	☐
3 Chris Ellison goes to the island by plane.	☐	☐
4 Chris thinks he sees somebody behind the trees.	☐	☐
5 There is a small hill near the megalithic stone.	☐	☐
6 The American woman says she is working on the island.	☐	☐
7 The American woman is friendly.	☐	☐
8 Chris does not like where he lives.	☐	☐

2 Why do these things happen?

1 The people on the island do not like archaeologists. Why?
   Choose one answer.

   a ☐ Because archaeologists take things from tombs.

   b ☐ Because the megalithic stones are very important
      for them.

   c ☐ Because the people on the island are doing
      something bad with the stones.

2 A tree falls in front of the car. Why? Choose one answer.

  a ☐ Because the tree is very old.

  b ☐ Because somebody wants to kill Chris.

  c ☐ Because somebody does not want Chris to go to his house.

3 What happens next? Complete the sentences.

  1 The next day . . .

  a ☐ Chris studies some megalithic stones.

  b ☐ he stays at home.

  c ☐ he talks to people in the town.

  2 Somebody . . .

  a ☐ tells Chris a lot of things about the megalithic stones.

  b ☐ tries to kill Chris.

  c ☐ helps Chris find a tomb.

  3 The American woman . . .

  a ☐ wants to help Chris.

  b ☐ wants Chris to go home to England.

  4 The people on the island . . .

  a ☐ help Chris.

  b ☐ don't help Chris.

  5 Later near the megalithic stones Chris finds . . .

  a ☐ a tomb.

  b ☐ a dead person.

  c ☐ a very old knife.

After Reading

1 Answer these questions.

1 Who does Chris meet on the ferry?

2 Where is the American woman's house?

3 What does Chris see on the door of his house?

4 When Chris is driving to Clayonag he sees something behind him. What is it?

5 Chris sees something under the car. What is it?

6 There are some boxes near the stones. What does Chris see in the boxes?

7 Who do the police arrest?

2 A policeman is asking Chris some questions. Put the words in the correct order. Then write the answers to the questions.

1 are where from you?

....

....

2 do what do you?

....

....

3 you why on are the island?

....

....

4 staying are where you ?

....

....

5 is who tall the man?

....

....

3 Match the sentence halves to make eight complete sentences.

1 The American woman wants Chris to …
2 The American woman does not want Chris to …
3 The tall man is helping …
4 The tall man hits Chris's car with a stone because …
5 Clayonag is …
6 When the sun shines into the door, the people …
7 The man works on the car for a …
8 The American woman does not see that …

a begin to sing.
b long time.
c near the sea.
d the American woman.
e go to Clayonag.
f the stone is falling.
g see the treasure.
h Chris is coming home early.

ABOUT THE AUTHOR

Lester Vaughan was born in England. When he was young he travelled around Europe, South America, and the Middle East. He now lives in Murcia in southern Spain where he teaches English. He also teaches at Hilderstone College in England. He has published five books and also works on the Oxford English File series. In his free time Lester enjoys painting, cycling, and t'ai chi.

OXFORD BOOKWORMS LIBRARY

Classics • Crime & Mystery • Factfiles • Fantasy & Horror
Human Interest • Playscripts • Thriller & Adventure
True Stories • World Stories

The OXFORD BOOKWORMS LIBRARY provides enjoyable reading in English, with a wide range of classic and modern fiction, non-fiction, and plays. It includes original and adapted texts in seven carefully graded language stages, which take learners from beginner to advanced level. An overview is given on the next pages.

All Stage 1 titles are available as audio recordings, as well as over eighty other titles from Starter to Stage 6. All Starters and many titles at Stages 1 to 4 are specially recommended for younger learners. Every Bookworm is illustrated, and Starters and Factfiles have full-colour illustrations.

The OXFORD BOOKWORMS LIBRARY also offers extensive support. Each book contains an introduction to the story, notes about the author, a glossary, and activities. Additional resources include tests and worksheets, and answers for these and for the activities in the books. There is advice on running a class library, using audio recordings, and the many ways of using Oxford Bookworms in reading programmes. Resource materials are available on the website <www.oup.com/bookworms>.

The *Oxford Bookworms Collection* is a series for advanced learners. It consists of volumes of short stories by well-known authors, both classic and modern. Texts are not abridged or adapted in any way, but carefully selected to be accessible to the advanced student.

———————————————

You can find details and a full list of titles in the *Oxford Bookworms Library Catalogue* and *Oxford English Language Teaching Catalogues*, and on the website <www.oup.com/bookworms>.

THE OXFORD BOOKWORMS LIBRARY
GRADING AND SAMPLE EXTRACTS

present simple – present continuous – imperative –
can/cannot, must – *going to* (future) – simple gerunds …

Her phone is ringing – but where is it?

Sally gets out of bed and looks in her bag. No phone. She looks under the bed. No phone. Then she looks behind the door. There is her phone. Sally picks up her phone and answers it. ***Sally's Phone***

STAGE 1 • 400 HEADWORDS

… past simple – coordination with *and, but, or* – subordination with *before, after, when, because, so* …

I knew him in Persia. He was a famous builder and I worked with him there. For a time I was his friend, but not for long. When he came to Paris, I came after him – I wanted to watch him. He was a very clever, very dangerous man. ***The Phantom of the Opera***

STAGE 2 • 700 HEADWORDS

… present perfect – *will* (future) – *(don't) have to, must not, could* – comparison of adjectives – simple *if* clauses – past continuous – tag questions – *ask/tell* + infinitive …

While I was writing these words in my diary, I decided what to do. I must try to escape. I shall try to get down the wall outside. The window is high above the ground, but I have to try. I shall take some of the gold with me – if I escape, perhaps it will be helpful later. ***Dracula***

... should, may – present perfect continuous – *used to* – past perfect – causative – relative clauses – indirect statements ...

Of course, it was most important that no one should see Colin, Mary, or Dickon entering the secret garden. So Colin gave orders to the gardeners that they must all keep away from that part of the garden in future. ***The Secret Garden***

STAGE 4 • 1400 HEADWORDS
... past perfect continuous – passive (simple forms) – *would* conditional clauses – indirect questions – relatives with *where/when* – gerunds after prepositions/phrases ...

I was glad. Now Hyde could not show his face to the world again. If he did, every honest man in London would be proud to report him to the police. ***Dr Jekyll and Mr Hyde***

STAGE 5 • 1800 HEADWORDS
... future continuous – future perfect – passive (modals, continuous forms) – *would have* conditional clauses – modals + perfect infinitive ...

If he had spoken Estella's name, I would have hit him. I was so angry with him, and so depressed about my future, that I could not eat the breakfast. Instead I went straight to the old house. ***Great Expectations***

STAGE 6 • 2500 HEADWORDS
... passive (infinitives, gerunds) – advanced modal meanings – clauses of concession, condition

When I stepped up to the piano, I was confident. It was as if I knew that the prodigy side of me really did exist. And when I started to play, I was so caught up in how lovely I looked that I didn't worry how I would sound. ***The Joy Luck Club***

BOOKWORMS · CRIME & MYSTERY · STARTER

Oranges in the Snow

PHILLIP BURROWS AND MARK FOSTER

'Everything's ready now. We can do the experiment,' says your assistant Joe.

You are the famous scientist Mary Durie working in a laboratory in Alaska. When you discover something very new and valuable, other people want to try to steal your idea – can you stop them before they escape?

BOOKWORMS · HUMAN INTEREST · STARTER

Survive!

HELEN BROOKE

You are in a small plane, going across the Rocky Mountains. Suddenly, the engine starts to make strange noises . . .

Soon you are alone, in the snow, at the top of a mountain, and it is very, very cold. Can you find your way out of the mountain?

Drive into Danger

ROSEMARY BORDER

'I can drive a truck,' says Kim on her first day at work in the office. When Kim's passenger Andy finds something strange under the truck things get dangerous – very dangerous.

A Connecticut Yankee in King Arthur's Court

MARK TWAIN

Retold by Alan Hines

Hank Morgan is a happy young man in Connecticut, USA in 1879 until one day someone runs into his office and shouts, 'Come quickly, Boss! Two men are fighting.' After this, something very strange happens to him, and his life changes forever.

The Monkey's Paw

W. W. JACOBS

Retold by Diane Mowat

Outside, the night is cold and wet. Inside, the White family sits and waits. Where is their visitor?

There is a knock at the door. A man is standing outside in the dark. Their visitor has arrived.

The visitor waits. He has been in India for many years. What has he got? He has brought the hand of a small, dead animal – a monkey's paw.

Outside, in the dark, the visitor smiles and waits for the door to open.

The President's Murderer

JENNIFER BASSETT

The President is dead!

A man is running in the night. He is afraid and needs to rest. But there are people behind him – people with lights, and dogs, and guns.

A man is standing in front of a desk. His boss is very angry, and the man is tired and needs to sleep. But first he must find the other man, and bring him back – dead or alive.

Two men: the hunter and the hunted. Which will win and which will lose?

Long live the President!